D0014415

So You're
30!

Mike Haskins & Clive Whichelow

summersdale

SO YOU'RE 30!

Summersdale Publishers Ltd
46 West Street
Chichester
West Sussex
PO19 1RP
UK

www.summersdale.com

Printed and bound by Tien Wah Press, Singapore

ISBN: 978-1-84024-726-8

TO...

FROM...

INTRODUCTION

So you're 30! At last, you're mature. Well, mature-ish. You're not out clubbing every night any more, and thank goodness for that you may well think, because quite frankly it's rather knackering. Anyway, these days you've got other things to spend your money on – like trying to buy a house, or perhaps a flat, or maybe just a glorified bedsit. You need to get a foot on the property ladder, or at least a toe.

That's the thing when you reach 30 – you suddenly feel you should be doing more grown-up things. It's as if a little alarm in your body goes off, saying, 'Right! Time to start watching more property programmes on the TV, more makeover shows, more cookery...' In fact, time to start watching more TV full stop.

You suddenly start appreciating more relaxed pursuits such as country walks. You join the AA – the Automobile Association that is, not Alcoholics Anonymous. You begin to find that, on certain subjects, your parents may not have been talking complete rubbish after all. On the quiet you may even start to agree with some of their more extreme opinions.

But while the age on your birthday cards is desperately trying to tug you towards maturity, a little voice in the back of your head is saying, 'Rebel!' It's the little voice that tells you to have just one more drink, to wear shorts to the office, which says, 'Just because you're thirty there's no reason you shouldn't have a skateboard, a PlayStation or a pierced nipple.'

So you're 30! It's just 15 the second time around!

WHY 30 ISN'T REALLY THAT OLD

If you were a fine wine you'd still be considered a youngster.

You're still young enough to be bailed out by your parents.

You're unlikely to have a really grown-up job yet like high court judge or MP.

You haven't even considered Botox yet.

You've been allowed to drink legally for only 12 years.

WHY 30 REALLY IS THAT OLD

If you were a fine cheese you'd be
pretty pungent by now.

Drinking legally for 12 years has
prematurely aged your body
by more than 80 years.

You have to explain to youngsters
who Nirvana were.

If you were a computer you'd be
the size of a small house.

It's halfway to 60.

THE BASIC MYTHS ABOUT TURNING 30

Thirty is the new 20 – not according to any 20-year-olds it's not.

You now know where you're going in life – you don't even know where you're going tonight.

You're now a mature, responsible, independent adult – really? Even though you still rely on your dad to do any DIY and your mum to do your laundry?

You're now treated with more respect – but only by those who are trying to sell you something.

GIVEAWAYS THAT WILL TELL PEOPLE YOU ARE OVER 30

You've started wearing a crash helmet when skateboarding.

You can remember the Spice Girls when they really were girls.

You can split a restaurant bill without arguing over who had what.

A GUIDE TO HOW OTHERS WILL NOW PERCEIVE YOU

By teenagers: as a has-been now merely
of curiosity value

By bar owners: as someone who
probably won't smash the place up

By the opposite sex: as a bit suspicious if you're not yet spoken for

THE MAIN THINGS IN YOUR LIFE YOU WILL NOW LOOK FORWARD TO

Having a pet that isn't a hamster or a guinea pig

Becoming old enough to get nostalgic
about your youth

Being swamped with marriage offers
from peers who have started to panic
about being left on the shelf

THE MAIN THINGS IN YOUR LIFE IT'S LESS EASY TO LOOK FORWARD TO

Getting a little bit nearer to being 40 every day

Realising you look more like the 'before' than the 'after' picture in an ad for an anti-ageing product

Realising all your favourite music is now
on 'oldies' radio stations

STATISTICALLY SPEAKING

You have now been alive for about 262,974 hours. If you'd worked all of those, even at the minimum wage of £5.73 per hour, you could so far have amassed a fortune of £1,506,841. If you have made this fortune, congratulations! It must have been quite hard holding down a job as a newborn baby...

Thirty years is about 10,957 days. Doesn't sound that long, does it? Maybe that's why you haven't got much done yet. Especially as the last 4,382 days (i.e. since you turned 18) probably passed in a drunken blur.

You've made between 65,742
and 87,656 trips to the lavatory
(must be all that excitement).

So far your heart has beaten about 1,136,049,336 times (although this figure could be slightly higher depending on how exciting things have been).

You've slept around 76,699 hours (again this could be affected by how exciting a time you've been having).

And you've breathed in about 189,341,556 times (perhaps a bit less, depending on the condition of some of those lavatories you've been visiting on your exciting nights out).

All that in just 30 years! No wonder you're feeling so tired!

THINGS YOU HAVE TO SHOW
FOR YOUR 30 YEARS

A walk-in wardrobe full of nothing but
used wristbands from music festivals

An address book full of the phone numbers of girlfriends/boyfriends you had before you got your first mobile

A disease that you still haven't shaken off from that gap year in Asia

An encyclopaedic knowledge of every
club and bar within a 30-mile
radius of your home

A hangover destined to last as long as
the non-stop drinking binge
that was your twenties

The ability to text in your sleep

NOW YOU'RE 30 THE FOLLOWING WILL BE YOUR NATURAL ENEMIES

Young people who look like they're having a better time than you

Mortgage advisers who scoff at your meagre income

Friends who have become 'mature students' and regale you with tales of the fun they're still having

People who lie and say they're 29

THINGS YOU SHOULD HAVE ACHIEVED BY NOW

The ability to talk politely to members
of the opposite sex whom you
don't find attractive

Not boasting about how many points
you've got on your driving licence

Being able to get through a whole week
without eating a takeaway

THINGS YOU'LL FEEL
SMUG ABOUT

Not needing any cosmetic surgery (yet)

Having achieved all your school
qualifications without the aid
of the Internet

Being able to change a fuse without
having to call your dad for instructions

HOORAY! THINGS YOU'LL NEVER HAVE TO DO AGAIN

Be friends with someone just because of the range of computer games they own

Have your tent stolen while you're queuing for the toilets at a music festival

Tidy your room if you don't want to

Rely on mum and dad's taxi service

BOO! THINGS YOU WON'T BE DOING AGAIN

Going on another Club 18–30 holiday

Being slipped a bit of cash by an elderly relative so you can 'get yourself something nice'

Calling yourself a 'twenty-something'
(Well, you might still get away with it...)

Participating in any events that have
the word 'youth' in their title

AARGHH! THINGS YOU NEVER THOUGHT WOULD HAPPEN

You buy a piece of new technology
that you can't get to work.

You get asked to join the local neighbourhood watch.

You are mistaken for one of your parents.

THINGS TO EXPECT FOR YOUR NEXT BIRTHDAY

A car vac

A subscription to a home and garden magazine

A book entitled
Do You Remember the 1990s?

The same gifts you were
given this birthday

GADGETS THAT YOU MAY STILL OWN

An iPod from 2001 with a mechanical scroll wheel

A green screen Game Boy

A Rubik's cube
(which you still can't solve)

An original Sony Walkman
cassette player

BEING 30 IS...

... being too old for roller skates
but too young for rollers.

... being too old for ice creams but too
young for cream teas.

... being too old for acid house but too young for acid indigestion.

... being too old to be up and coming but too young to be down and out.

YOUR NEW OUTLOOK
ON LIFE

Your idea of a wild weekend is
visiting a safari park.

When you tell your friends how much
you drank last night it's in units
rather than cans.

The number of partners you've had
has become a source of worry
rather than boasting.

THINGS YOU WILL DESPERATELY TRY TO AVOID

Wearing 'comfy' clothes

Saying 'in my day...'

Having to 'come out' as a
James Blunt fan

Showing too much interest
in property prices

THOSE WERE THE DAYS!
NOSTALGIA FOR THE
OVER 30S

When 'social networking sites' were
known as nightclubs

When mobile phones were the size
and weight of a house brick and you
needed to be standing on top of
Ben Nevis to get a signal

When spam was something your
granddad had for his tea

When the only instant messaging you
did was with two old bean cans
and a piece of string

When Paris Hilton was a hotel

THINGS YOU'D BETTER DO IN YOUR 30S BEFORE IT'S TOO LATE

Establish once and for all exactly how much alcohol and food your body can handle in one sitting without unfortunate consequences

Master the art of having a proper
conversation with your mum or dad

Make your body a temple before it
becomes a chapel of rest

See the world while your eyesight
is still up to the job

Come up with some ingenious means
of paying off your student loan

BEHAVIOUR THAT ISN'T GOING TO LOOK GOOD IN YOUR 30S

Still trying to make it as a pop star

Taking your twelfth successive
gap year so far

Dating 17-year-olds

FASHION REVIVALS YOU CAN LOOK FORWARD TO

The 'baggy' look

Sucking a babies' dummy at a rave

The 'Rachel' hairdo

Smiley face T-shirts

Teenage Mutant Ninja Turtles costumes

YOU REALLY KNOW YOU'VE PASSED 30 WHEN...

... you first ask someone to turn their music down.

... the first page you turn to in the newspaper is the investments.

... you find the latest fashions
utterly ridiculous.

... items on your shopping list are all
prefixed with 'low sugar',
'fat free' or 'bran'.

THINGS YOU CAN NOW GET AWAY WITH THAT YOU COULDN'T PREVIOUSLY

Buying alcohol without showing your ID

Using an ATM without the words
'insufficient funds' coming
up on the screen

Going for a job interview without having to take your exam certificates with you in a plastic wallet

THINGS YOU ARE NOW LIKELY TO HAVE IN YOUR HOME

A bewildering array of kitchen gadgets

A massive TV for all those nights in watching repeats of *Friends*

A local free newspaper that you actually read

THINGS THAT YOU SHOULD NO LONGER HAVE IN YOUR HOME

Cans of spray paint –
unless you're Banksy

Spanish hotel towels

A microwave oven as your
sole cooking device

All your mates 'hanging out' and spilling
curry on your living room carpet

REASONS TO BE CHEERFUL

If you've survived your twenties,
you can survive anything.

Your adolescent acne might
finally be clearing up.

You're now indisputably a mature
adult, so yah boo sucks!

www.summersdale.com